Mary is a River

Mary is a River

Poems by

Rachel Jamison Webster

Kelsay Books

© 2018 Rachel Jamison Webster. All rights reserved. This material may not be reproduced in any form, published, reprinted, recorded, performed, broadcast, without the express written consent of Rachel Jamison Webster. All such actions are strictly prohibited by law.

Cover: Photo: "Ritual Bathing" by Vanessa Filley
Cover Design: John McCarthy

ISBN: 978-1-947465-82-4

Kelsay Books
Aldrich Press
www.kelsaybooks.com

Acknowledgements

Mary is a River was a finalist for the 2014 National Poetry Series.

I would like to thank those judges and also the editors of the journals who first published excerpts of this book.

Cumberland River Review

Dappled Things

Narrative Magazine

Spoon River Poetry Review

Contents

Part 1

1. I've been folded like a mushroom in the dirt	11
2. I dreamed, I slept. I traveled into the folds	12
3. I wake now with lime on my tongue, sputtering	13
4. I remember our bodies, how fragile they were	14
5. And sometimes, remembering like this	15
6. Then I think that's just a small way	16
7. I had not known I had been waiting	17
8. So I knew I'd know when I saw him	18
9. I stood shock-still, my breath	19
10. But when I came outside, he was gone—	20
11. When he walked through the others	21
12. So it began	22
13. Yet to say yes—took everything	23
14. I traveled with men who hated me	24
15. Those nights, I'd feel my hands and feet pinned	25
16. Then there would be some sign	26
17. I remember those first days	27
18. To be reborn of the spirit, the water	28
19. But how I trembled when I laid my hand	29
20. Before we met, I had dreams that portended	30
21. So most of my pilgrimage took place within	31
22. The new was unfolding the old	32
23. I remember their need like a hunger	33
24. We were woven into the dance	34
25. I remember we would lie together	35
26. After many weeks of this, connecting	36
27. Designs were always being revealed	37
28. There was a cynicism to our time	38
29. I was a woman, one of many	39
30. So always at the heart of my joy there was this	40

Part 2

31. I sleep the shallow sleep of the mystics now	43
32. Those days were my life	44
33. But what is more difficult to describe than bliss?	45
34. No man alone could have known	46
35. Our lives were our art, as they always are	48
36. I know the anger the living feel	50
37. It had been the strangest week	51
38. We were not where we needed to be	52
39. Afterward, I begged him	54
40. I found my feet. I ran after him	55
41. The next hours and days passed so slowly	56
42. What could I do then, but begin to live	57
43. Outside, I went to him and said one thing	59
44. That night he slept with me, and once again	60
45. On our last morning together, he woke	61
46. That evening was the supper, the false celebration	62
47. He spent that night alone	64
48. So by time's darkest morning	65
49. He was pinned to the limits	66
50. For a time, I had that body	68
51. Now, deep in the seams of sleep, pangs	69
52. Now, deep in the seams of sleep, pangs	70
53. All night my hands throbbed with messages	71
54. We wept	72
55. They did not believe me	73
56. I ache now from the core of the earth	74
57. After he died, my life became life	75
58. Do you remember the birds	76
59. Now I sit beside the river and watch water	77
60. We've burrowed in matter to its afterlife as light	79

Afterword
About the Author

Part 1

1.

I've been folded like a mushroom in the dirt.
I've been trapped like something dirty in the dirt.

I've hidden myself in layers of self,
folded into curtains and veils and mothering,

and now there is nothing left to do
but begin to tell—myself—the story.

I could say it all so simply.

I could say, once upon a time, I lived,
and my living was like divining.

The deeper I moved toward the truth of my life,
the wilder the wand of me sang and was sung.

I could say, I loved. And when I loved
even deserts beat in me like a sea.

2.

I dreamed, I slept. I traveled into the folds
of the earth and my hair thinned

and my body, until I became more
breath than form.

Only then did I begin my return
to the light that filters the world.

Speaking like this, thumbing for a stem
of truth, is like trying to find a fossil.

I locate the ridge where the vertebrae was,
and blow away the dust of stomach,

epistles, a village—and what
is underneath is not so much

a body, but a movement, a drum
of the blood. I step in again, become a river

stirring history's silt, sliding over stories
slick with sludge and moss.

I'll have to wear them down
to before he was, before I was.

Before we humans moved out
across the land in rivulets,

branching up and over
its cracked hand.

3.

I wake now with lime on my tongue, sputtering
the dry taste of time.

I wake now in my hands,
wondering which woman I am.

I wake outside my names.

Like water, I slip into them,
I go where I am needed.

Like a woman,
I go where I am needed.

I flow the slope and carve slowly
rock and mud under growing grass,

I move and in movement recall
our work, our hands in flashes—

Then I think back to before that story, to the sky
that split open over my own birth.

I see those tides of stars and wonder
where we are. And how did I—

who may have been a bird or limb
or cave molting the age-old salt and rime—

how did I become a woman?
How did I become a woman who loved a man

who became more than a man?
Was I more than a woman?

4.

I remember our bodies, how fragile they were
through all of it, by being bodies, how young.

Sun sifted into the skin of our wrists
and glittered up in its geometries.

It raised us from dirt into our limbs
and our hands, our hands

became balms and tutors and birds.
They led us like strange elders.

We spoke so many languages with our hands!
They strummed us up into knowing

the being that needed release.

5.

And sometimes, remembering like this,
waiting for my voice to thicken,

I think, we were just children

born so sensitive we chafed
against the world.

I think, we were just children.

So terrified of death
we had to make ourselves myths.

6.

Then I think that's just a small way
to tell the story, a summary.

If we were children, we were
also sand stinging the children's eyes,

calling up water to swaddle flaw into pearl,
heal the eye by making it cry.

If we were sand, we were also the wind
carrying sand, also the tides conversing

with the wind. Understand,
it was abstract even as it was happening.

I could feel myself quickening
into the life of the spirit.

7.

I had not known I had been waiting
for anything. As a girl, I had awakened

every morning in destiny's hot eye, but lately
I had felt that gaze widen and retract

from me. I had learned more deeply
the ways of women, growing golder,

becoming slowly wheat in a field of wheat.
We, we, we wove the work

of the seasons, and in our chattering
waves of generations, in the wide webbing

roots between us, I knew my destiny
was ours. So I had what I needed.

And I had something else,
like a stone or glow, suspended

somewhere beneath my breastbone.
And I could visit it, not like a place,

but like a musical tuning—
to see if it were balanced in me.

In this way, I lived.
In this way, I knew through my body

the currents of our time.

8.

So I knew I'd know when I saw him
if he was what they said:

a teacher, a messenger, a son of man.

I stood at the gate to watch him pass,
and he saw me. He became the first person

ever really to see me. And I felt him,
his goodness, immediately.

It was beyond what I had called human.

It is what is possible for the human
who has given up smallness.

9.

I stood shock-still, my breath
leaving me for the wind.

I was stunned, then embarrassed
by my own surprise, which I felt was a lack

of preparation. So I went inside to get something,
anything, to give him, but I thought then

that even my gift would be evidence
of my unworthiness.

I saw how then how we humans hide
our shame in our belongings.

I grabbed the jar of finest oil
because I wanted him to be recognized.

But also because I wanted to free myself
from the wealth that had contained me in the world.

See, immediately, my love was
buffeted by my thinking.

Immediately, everything was
upside-down and righted.

10.

But when I came outside, he was gone—
up the way, talking to a gathering crowd.

So I, who did not follow, followed.
I, who usually led, stood at the back

and listened. And I lived each minute
as a pained exiled lifetime

in which I thought I had missed
my opportunity to learn his true name.

I did not hear a word he said that day.
But I saw his breath filling his body,

his body that was shining.

And tears coursed down my face
like the rivers that throb under wheat.

11.

When he walked through the others
to me, I thought, God is simply *mercy*.

From the beginning, I saw in him
divinity mingled with man,

and I saw that both had been lonely.

So I anointed him, as if to say,
I'll serve you by seeing you.

Everyone else saw too.
But how? How could a woman

be so base and so audacious at once?
So they mixed and muddled me,

made me into no woman, two women, three,
because what one woman could

contain such contradiction—

and believe me it roiled through my body
like a wail, like the birth scream of centuries,

I shook all over with it—the shame and bravery
intertwined, which is love.

12.

So it began.

Everything I had ever known or done
had been only a preparation

for the moment I was in.
When I leveled my eyes to meet his.

When I tore off household and husband
to enter the world with him, huskless and shy.

When I left my life for my life.

I learned to trust everything I knew
and everything I did not yet know.

I learned the divine would reach in
to meet me, the way the sea slides in

to meet, and shape, the shore.

13.

Yet to say yes—took everything.

It was a stepping out into air, peerless,
without ground—

Understand, it was all new.

I had only intuition and faith
to steady a way beneath me.

I did not yet have these comforts,
and specters, of memory.

14.

I traveled with men who hated me
and women who feared for me.

And at times, terror moved through me
in its tumult of strings.

Fear changed the music in me,
which was confusing, because I knew

fear was doing enough
damage in the world.

Those nights, I would wish I had not been chosen,
forgetting that I too had chosen.

My body would go so cold,
the shoals of the dark would roll on

so long and so deep, I would see myself
as just a single frozen bone, rattling on the sands.

I would think that by walking away
from my old life, I had chosen

the life of a story, a ghost,
and I would never again get warm.

15.

Those nights, I'd feel my hands and feet pinned
to their singular places, as if nailed

by iron, hard-hooked and hooking
again into earth, stiffening to stone,

cold departing my bones
in heavy slow-coursing roots.

But mornings, my palms would wake first,
and over their pulsing, I'd trace

a triangle up and a triangle down
in the ancient open star.

In this way, I'd pray
to use my hands right.

16.

Then there would be some sign.
I would dream the village we would reach the next day.

Or we'd meet a traveling family and somehow
I would know all of their names.

In some small way, I would be of use.
So my faith in him was always part

of a larger faith. And Love,
which was beyond us,

was always taking us past where
we thought our lives would go.

17.

I remember those first days.
We were so busy, we were both leaders.

We would look across at one another.

Our feet would bleed from walking,
our tongues would thicken and our lips

would crack from the dust
and the sun and discussions.

And nights would descend on us heavily
as crowns, settling cool silver on our hair and brows.

We would look across at one another.

I would watch him over the fire
as we ate and imagine my hand

was his hand, feeding me.

18.

To be reborn of the spirit, the water,
to be changed in the fluidity of change.

I thought of water as that grass all around us,
rolling on in waves, over sand carved

by recessions of waves, over land
that remembers being underwater,

the way a man remembers a woman.
I walked that land with him as water,

one and mingling, breaking into breath and sweat,
passing on even as we were passing through.

I remember sitting with him once by the sea,
sifting in and out of conversation,

watching the waves curl forward and in sudden
clarity slide back again, bubble-fringed, over sand.

For a moment, the wave was the sand
and the sand was the wave.

And they wanted to be.

19.

But how I trembled when I laid my hand
on his head, on the warm

quiver that was his hair and my knees
dipped and my stomach swam into sun

and what wouldn't I give to the one
who needed me like that?

20.

Before we met, I had dreams that portended
what we lived together.

And in my own dreams it was difficult
to tell what was fear and what was truth.

It was like untangling a knotted bunch
of bright strings. Some fears unraveled

into truths, and some truths twisted into fears
in the way we lived them.

In one, we were walking through
pastures hung with a red sun and full moon,

and between this floating stone and floating fire,
we walked, ourselves floating footless in grass.

I understood we had been walking
toward one another for many years.

We could go on walking in a repetition
of the generations, or we could walk beside

this other we had dreamed. But to do so
meant we would lose our names.

It meant my life would not belong to me.

21.

So most of my pilgrimage took place within.

I wandered the deserts and shorelines
and labyrinthine markets of my own heart.

I traveled long and thirstily toward
my own face, toward my belief

that I would pass through it and see
from its eyes the other, my other,

when I was ready. And then
there would be no other.

22.

The new was unfolding the old
from within in the inevitable pleasures

the snake feels shedding its skin,
or a lake knows, turning over,

exchanging the cold panes of the deep
for the sun-strummed running surface.

I could breathe through the net of me,
feel the wind through the sieve of my skin—

I could feel myself a vessel,
and I was happy.

23.

I remember their need like a hunger
in the air, drawing us up into sustenance.

Everywhere we went, people
needed us like that. And we knew each one

in the eyes as the wound and its antidote,
the shadow as the shape of its glow.

We showed them to themselves
in love and they saw truth

would hold them, they would not die.
Knowing themselves whole

was what healed them.
And us? What healed us

was the work, becoming
the bright limbs of one being.

24.

We were woven into the dance
of it, a rising hope we were

rising like a tent of silk and silk rope we were
being lifted beyond our own hands.

I liked to stand silent as he spoke,
a listening wand, a rod to the ground.

I have left the tent of women,
I thought, to become one,

my bones the supporting stakes,
my skin the tarp, my heart the hearth,

and trembling then at the edges of my form.

25.

I remember we would lie together
and I would slide into sleep

through both of our bodies
slipping as if under water,

gradually unknowing
which was his hand which was mine

and which a hand at all.

26.

After many weeks of this, connecting,
reconnecting, I had some time alone.

I took a cloth and lay under a tree
and my sight fluttered at the edges,

and I was the tree, shaking in wind,
drinking light to my tips.

I was the rooted ringing wood
and each delighted leaf.

When I woke with the sun in my eye,
he was over me, gazing down,

running a blade of grass
along my cheek. And I knew then

that we had known eternity.
There we are a brook of leaves.

27.

Designs were always being revealed
by way of higher designs.

He led us, and he stirred up humans like dust.

All those questions. The way they were always
trying to trip him up with rules and traditions.

They believed him on sight—
I watched them ruffle with recognition—

then worked backward, collecting reasons
not to believe like coins, vouchsafing doubt.

Meanwhile, we saw so much
of the world is a corpse-world.

We lived the reality that is
always alive, always changing

us to nothing, to something,
to the spirit's sown seeds.

28.

There was a cynicism to our time,

with violence's constant simmer
and a glaze over the eyes.

It was much like your time.

Fear had bled into the waters.
We had been nursed on worry.

The eyes of the world saw the part
and not the whole.

The eyes of the world were dividing eyes,
hooked on ornaments and forms.

But just as the faithful seem stupid
to the faithless, so do the faithless

seem blind to the faithful.
We knew that love begets

love, fear begets fear, strength
begets strength.

That this is what it means
to be the living word.

29.

I was a woman, one of many.

I had waited in my mother
while she grew in hers, my unborn daughter

waited in me, the spheres of her daughters
in her, and we went on like this, worlds

without end, needing only to be ignited in love
to unfold from the whole into selves.

Was this not already greatness?
What was in a name?

How could I not see martyrdom
as a kind of terror, alienation or shame?

30.

So always at the heart of my joy there was this
deep and bleating grief.

It did not so much foresee his end
but keen with the trick of mortality.

To become this conscious
just to lose your life?

To love to completion
just to lose your love?

I had never seen anyone love as we did,
and I thought it would break me and it did.

I began to understand the way
women are broken into motherhood.

The body does it for you,
you have no choice, you are opened,

and the old life leaves you with the waters
and the skins of the waters.

You die and are reborn
in your tether to another.

And in the child's sleep, which remembers
the warm surrounding body,

and in the child's helplessness,
you come to know your own.

I marveled at this, at the courage
of those who love.

Part 2

31.

I sleep the shallow sleep of the mystics now,
in thin blankets of time.

I sleep just to wake, eyes shivering my lids,
my hands radiating outward.

They are like stars, throbbing
because staked to their places.

I too am throbbing, troubled
by all I have not said.

But where, again, should I begin?

There is nothing like being alive.
The beauty of it. Colors and light

strumming colors. Tastes shuddering
into color on the tongue.

All those connections always
coursing through you!

And though there are brighter and brighter
realms, you can only reach them by living.

32.

Those days were my life.

Eating apricots warm from the orchards,
bits of salted fish.

My hair when I moved, releasing
the scent of woodsmoke.

How softly we would sing, setting out
on clay roads as the sun rose,

our stopped talk calming the dust,
the soft sounds of us, singing.

And the light! Clear patterings
through the leaves, playing trembling notes

on the faces. Need and hope flickering
in the faces of the people.

Then truth like clean rain breaking over us.

Truth like a wind and sudden rapidity
in which we could feel again, and see.

Those days, it was as if
the very sun was loving us.

Our future was opening flawlessly as a blossom
in a sea of nodding blossoms.

We were alive in the moment we were becoming.

33.

But what is more difficult to describe than bliss?

Bliss by being bliss belies specifics
and is impossible to express

in the arc of a story, which always chronicles
what was once and now is gone.

The story's slivering is a lie,
its ordering of time, a lie,

an alabaster box designed by our minds
to contain what's beyond time.

We did not live days.
We lived one undivided eternity.

When we were alive, we knew that
time was just a story we played at.

For a time.

34.

No man alone could have known
what he knew about love without his own love.

But in the stories, he was made singular
and I was blurred into plural.

I became the server, the whore,
the sister of the risen, a girl

plural as the furrowed fields.

For some, I was a jug
broken and buried in sand,

a shattered matrimony only some
had imagined.

I was just a coin
tendered through the ages—

one side a whore, the other a mother.

So you see why I, who was cut
and renamed in the stories, distrust stories.

I'll call our story a single shared
breath, spiraling into time,

or a song with contradiction as its bridge
and the contradiction was this:

I loved his work, which was mine,
and when he died, we were married

to the work, which he'd called God,
which spun God to one outside of us.

See there are many ways to tell this story.
There are many ways he and I

have been apart.

35.

Our lives were our art, as they always are
with beings of the spirit.

We lived in coincidence, synchronous
movement until meanings

rose from our motion like steam
from our breathing.

And when his life ended
with its terrible climaxing death,

all became art
and art's endless imitations.

We have been living under that tarp
of the sky for thousands of years.

They raised him high in his humility,
and they entombed me in my grief,

and my mouth filled with dust
and I choked on invisibility.

Anger became my apocrypha,
the part of me I could never express,

never condone. Each time I tried,
my tongue was torn, my back whipped or burned.

So it flowed up through the ages in red.
It glittered in windows and legends

where my hair wore the anger
my mouth could not share.

It glowed blood-warm and gold,
an iron halo.

36.

I know the anger the living feel
when their loved one is robbed

from them, anger when their own work
is stolen with that end.

And so women go crazy over wars,
because all along—as mother, sister, wife—

our work has been to weave him
more deeply into life.

But this is not a general thing.

This is my own wound.

37.

It had been the strangest week.

I was confused with a fear
that slushed to a mud in my mind.

On the day of the palm fronds
and hosannas, I watched

as they turned him into some kind
of circus act.

It was terrifying, it was not praise—
true praise is shy—but the wild

hunger of a crowd, and all a crowd wants
is to see something, anything,

that will relieve them of the boredom
of being merely themselves.

I watched, and like that first day,
I cried without knowing I was crying.

People waved branches, they chanted
and reached out to touch him,

a woman shoved me so hard I fell,
as I walked behind, doing nothing

but praying that I could protect him.
And I could not protect him.

38.

We were not where we needed to be.
He was happy—something in him

had needed that adulation—but distant from me.
Once I had guided us, but now

I felt his attention turning away
from me, and I lost my balance.

I switched back and back again.
What was truth and what was fear?

Could fear of his death
bring about his death?

Already he was hiding from me
in the folds of his disciples.

I don't trust this praise, I told them.
We should leave for a time, go North

and continue doing our work.
But everyone looked at me

like I was just a woman, and kept talking.
I can feel it, I said.

We are not in the right place.
But everyone thought I just wanted

to keep him small, to hold him
longer, the way a mother does.

I was made the righteous one alone then—
so I did become a mother.

I was the one who needed to believe
that our work and our lives could continue.

39.

Afterward, I begged him
to see what I had seen.

But he no longer really saw me.
Once, we had been one another's fate,

but now he had seen another fate,
a wager he had not tried to change.

He placed his hand on my head then,
and it was worse than a slap.

It said, she knows not what she does,
she knows me not.

I boiled with the rage of the ages then,
an anger so deep most women call it grief.

40.

I found my feet. I ran after him
and swung him around and sobbed

through my tears and my spit,
I will not let you die on my watch.

It is not your watch, he said.

I folded then, and I screamed.
I pressed my knuckles into the ground

until they cut and bled, stinging with sand.
I felt in his refusal of me

that we had left eternity for a
one-sided stitching into history, his story.

41.

The next hours and days passed so slowly.
I was muffled by confusion and grief.

How was I to stay awake just to see him suffer,
just to lose my love and my faith?

I swear I saw it all when the warrant came.
I saw him strung up on a symbol and used

like a lamb. I saw blood on the hands
that would shackle his wrists and shackle

his words and his acts.
I had participated in those acts,

and they were miraculous and startling
and often strangely funny, an inner drumming

ringing out from any motion we could see.
Now I saw their end, the shape and the whole

of them, as if they could be told,
as if the life they had sprung from

had not been a life,
but a parable for other people's use.

Once, he was not a story
belonging to everyone.

He was my beloved. But now this
was receding even with me in it.

42.

What could I do then, but begin to live
more wholly in the spirit?

Worldless currency that figures
in air and the deeps of earth and sea,

the spirit that is darkness and light,
mercurial and always extreme.

It was a kind of pulling back then,
an attempt to read the pattern

as if I were not of the pattern.
I began to memorize him—

how he sat with his soft shoulders,
how he lifted his glass, delicately,

the way his soft eyes darkened
as they listened, seeing more,

always more, than he would say.
I stared into every hair, my pain-edged eyes

ruffled every fringe and curl,
as I tried to hold his voice,

the rich, specific timbre of his voice.
It was his voice, I knew,

that would leave me first.
I noticed many of us staring

at him like that, with need
and disbelief pulling at our faces.

And never had these men, these brave men,
seemed so foolish to me—

the way they believed so credulously
in other men, the way they had convinced

themselves that we were powerful, safe,
the way they let him go like that unto death.

Now none of them could help him.
He would have find his faith within.

He would have to be alone with his God.

43.

Outside, I went to him and said one thing,
Do not be afraid.

He was so afraid.

Then I said, I know
our Father will hold you.

It felt false in my mouth
and I regretted the fact

that we had not used the word
Mother for God.

I could have said Mother,
I could have been that mother for a time.

I wanted only one thing—
to make him less afraid,

to give him the strength to bear
what he would have to bear.

I did not know how he would bear it.

44.

That night he slept with me, and once again
we entered the cairns of eternity.

I felt the lochs of my body opening,
my body in its liquid lifting,

and our eyes swimming so far
into one another they became one eye.

We traveled so long, into realms and colors
not yet beheld in our spectrum.

Again, I had known him.

Again, I had traveled into him
and him into me to know one another,

to know why we had come.

45.

On our last morning together, he woke
before me.

I thought then that he was the part of the body
that would have to die. And I was the part

that would have to live, to stay back alone
in the slower realm of stone and story.

In the seam between worlds,
that moment lasts forever.

I lived the remainder of my days
half in that moment.

I'd sleep to dip back in.

But that day, we were out of it, quickly.
He was rising into his courage.

And I was rising into some way to live
without him, wondering already

how I could describe him,
that Father, as I try to now.

46.

That evening was the supper, the false celebration
I could hardly stand—all of them nodding

about Heaven and the Kingdom of God,
as if it were simply the next stop on our travels.

Talking as if we were joining him,
when we knew we were letting him go alone.

I could not believe he was feeding us
in his hour of need.

He was placid and not pretending
to know more than he knew.

He was sitting still at the axis of mystery,
the crux of life and death.

And he spent the evening
inducting us again into metaphor,

saying the wine was his blood,
the bread was his body.

I choked on that when I realized
no one knew his body like I did, not even him.

He wanted us to remember
that we were one body,

that what passes through the body,
and the body itself is only a passing

and not the ever-living whole.

I knew this. I had always known this.
But that night, looking at his body

which would suffer and die,
and praying with mine

which held some of his life, I felt it.
I felt life's singularity.

I would know no other love.
He would have no other body.

And I marveled at this.
At the shape my love had taken.

47.

He spent that night alone
with his fear and his faith.

We each spend that night alone.

And I came through my weeping
to a desperate kind of questioning.

I asked what more I could have done
to protect him, and I asked what God

would do to protect him.
I asked for the truth to be enough for me,

and I asked for more than the truth.

I stayed awake to that tragedy
that before it is tragedy, is terror.

48.

So by time's darkest morning,
I had resolved to say goodbye

to his body, with faithful, fervent insistence
that I would know his spirit always.

I cut through the crowds to give him water.
What could they do to me now?

I chanted and sang my prayers as breath,
a bridge of breath I hoped would help him

leave his pain to enter the next heaven.
I sang of the resurrection of spring

and the promise of generations,
of wheat and of wheat and of wheat.

I walked beside him, and I felt his shoulders
as my shoulders—their burn, their ache

and their burden. It was the burden
of betrayal, of him and of us.

It was the betrayal of those we had healed,
by those we had trusted.

It was the betrayal of the God we had loved
that we thought had loved us.

It was the betrayal of the individual life
to its individual end.

It was so bitter,
and so common.

49.

He was pinned to the limits,
strung up on the scaffold

of separateness.
He was nailed to their death.

He was disgraced.
His face seized and became not his face.

His names fell away,
and his life in his pain.

They tortured him, and he suffered
so terribly I could not see it

singly. I watched him and watching
needed to believe that he watched himself

suffering, knew his body from beyond
as ours and his pain became that of all people

through time, echoing the before and after
to relieve us of suffering.

Then seeing him see himself
became an affront to me.

I had been attached to him as a man,
but life watching life is a winged thing.

Next time, I thought, it will be different.
We will not need such pain

in order to learn. He will be the woman,
I will be the man, it will not matter,

the matter we're in
will matter less.

In those awful hours that haunt
all hours, he became the prince

and the lamb, the pinnacle and lamp.
While in great reverberations of pain,

I became the mother and beloved,
sister and daughter. Any nameless one

who loves and cannot save her love.

50.

For a time, I had that body
I loved back in my arms.

I kissed the sludge of blood
from his brow, and saw it was ours.

We bathed him and oiled him.
We rubbed his skin and blessed him

for the journey he'd make away from us.
And it was a wonder—how small he was.

He could stir crowds and calm the waters,
but he'd been in a fragile, finite form all along.

Oh, it tore me open when they tore him from me.

They pried my limbs from his, and carried him
into the cave, the earth-womb, the tomb.

51.

Now, deep in the seams of sleep, pangs
come to me, asking, is it too late to awaken?

They come as thorns and nails come,
interrupting the flesh with memories

of what has harmed the flesh.
They come, asking, how could we

lose one another? Could I have said Mother
every time he said Father?

Could I have insisted I was more than a rib?
These questions clatter and cleave me in two.

I am the soul who knows and who knew.
And I am the woman who loved the man,

who saw genius become glory and celebration
persecution, and anger distend into sadness.

And who now must see it all back again.

52.

I pray and prayer ferries me,
and somehow the stone is rolled away.

I am hollow now as history, hollow as that tomb,
my throat slick with riversilt.

I can taste him in my mouth again.

I can taste the false perfumes
they spread on his ascension.

Answers come from either direction, therefore
unanswerable, and a buffeting shakes my skull,

and I wait.

53.

All night my hands throbbed with messages,
my brow twisted like rope with the signals.

I felt him surrounding me as he had in life,
but larger now, free.

I rose before dawn and went to the cave
to pray, but he was gone.

I ran to get help, and found someone,
a gardener. He watched me talk and did not move.

Do you recognize me? he asked.
Was it him already in the shape of any stranger?

Mary, he said. We beheld each other
and we were not afraid.

Who we had been were garments
of this we were becoming, a shimmering

emanation of the being we were
and ever would be, complete.

You cannot touch me, he said.

54.

We wept.

55.

They did not believe me,
but it was true. The tomb was empty.

They had stolen him and he had broken
into the light of world.

What he left was an opening
in the earth, a portal

for the human possibility
of divinity, anyone can enter.

56.

I ache now from the core of the earth,
water-carved tunnels aglow with what

the body knows. I loved him
to the point of losing myself, as if love

were the only truth. And when that love
destroyed me, its seeing restored me

in candlelit inlets of vision.

57.

After he died, my life became life
lived alongside the memory of life,

as world becomes word,
an aerating stream

in which the world's meaning
must again and again be remade.

Now I speak from the vestige of a name
that changed and changed,

with borrowed breath and bits of bone.
Now I speak of the world from the word.

Like sounds called out over water,
it is waveringly alive.

Like images cut from colored glass,
it is allegorically alive.

It is only as wide as your own life—
that bridge you have for a time.

Live there. Do not try
to enter the next realm until you are called.

But when you are called,
and whither, do follow.

58.

Do you remember the birds
threading the streets like spirits

through the sleeves of air?
Sunlight playing its iridescent scales

on the waves? Do you remember stepping in
to that water and letting it hold you?

Do you remember the waves breaking
around you, and afterward,

the shock of skin, the world
now without him?

Remember you stepped in
and in and into that river,

and it rushed you under and
delivered you, shining.

59.

Now I sit beside the river and watch
ripples scraped white by the light.

On one bank are basalt boulders. On the other,
smooth sand that once was such boulders.

Between them, two girls play,
their hair slick as the stones.

Again and again, they dive from the brim.
Again and again, they emerge.

One is broad-shouldered and sure.
The other is younger and follows.

They are playing with their father,
who is dark-skinned, with white hair

that sparks from his arms like cedars
and branches, the charged nerves of the earth.

He watches his daughters as they kick off
from the rocks and vanish in fizzing veils.

Watch this! they call.
Again and again, he watches.

Then he goes under—to rest or to test them.
He disappears in rings in rings in rings.

The daughters laugh.
Come back! they call,

until the green repairing surface
no longer remembers him.

They begin yelling then, his name
a terrified question.

60.

We've burrowed in matter to its afterlife as light.

We've discovered caverns in lime, connecting passages
of time. We've passed through channels

the water has made, as the mind
passes through its understandings.

And all this time, that life—
in its fast flash of presence

and long aftermath of sleep—
was only a day.

And I have had only one longing:
to get back to the wholeness

we were and we are.
Knowing I am in you as you are in me.

Selah.

Afterword

I remember being a girl sitting in my Protestant Church and listening to Bible passages filled with various Marys. "They didn't even bother to remember their real names," I'd think. I could open the Bible to whole pages of male lineages, but half of the women around Jesus—including his illustrious mother—were called "Mary," like a plural shorthand for "woman," or the generalized "Betty" of my own childhood's skater culture. Yet there she was, again and again, in all the most important moments: when he was anointed as The Christ, when he was murdered, when he was discovered missing from the tomb. So by the time Dan Brown's "The DaVinci Code" and Elaine Pagel's translations of the Gostic Gospels posited the idea that Mary Magdalene was not only Jesus's disciple but his wife, this idea seemed to me not only plausible but familiar, something I'd almost intuited. The enormous popularity of these books and others about Mary Magdalene indicate our own time's need to revisit and right Mary's story—not only historically, but metaphorically, as an example of the sacred feminine.

Evidence suggests that Mary Magdalene was a powerful woman from Magdala, a town on the Sea of Galilee, who traveled as one of Jesus' most trusted disciples. She may have been from a prominent Jewish family—like Jesus himself—and was likely a spiritual adept. As such a leader, she would have been a fitting partner for Jesus, able to grasp his radical teachings and provide listening, understanding and guidance. We do know that she continued to teach after Jesus's crucifixion, moving to France where she embodied and explained their philosophy, while living in prayer and spiritual community. French legend has it that she lived monastically, in caves and dwellings built into a mountain, where she developed inner seeing and clairvoyance.

In the first three centuries after Jesus' crucifixion, numerous sects of Christianity flourished, each interpreting his life and teachings differently. Among these interpretations was Gnosticism, an offshoot of Jewish spirituality that professed that people can know connection to the divine through "gnosis"—inner knowing or "knowledge of the heart." The Gnostics' abstract and often elaborate cosmology feminizes divinity and frequently mentions Mary Magdalene and the gospel that she taught in the years after Jesus' death. The Gnostics were considered heretics by early Church fathers and all writings associated with them, including the Gospels of Mary, Thomas and Philip, were banned from the New Testament in 325 C.E. after the Council of Nicaea. The Emperor Constantine presided at the Council, and 300 Bishops—referred to as the patriarchs—attended from every region of the Roman Empire. This was the first of many meetings that merged Christianity with politics and decreed legally enforceable standards of belief determined by the patriarchy.

After this meeting, all the books that mentioned Mary Magdalene's teachings were banned from the Bible. She was dangerous as an example of a powerful female teacher, a priestess, and as the woman that the Gnostic gospels say Jesus "loved more than all the other disciples." Any suggestion of their matrimony was repressed in order to assert Jesus' divinity over his humanity and to ideologically support the church, which was systematically dependent on celibacy.

Still, the character of Mary Magdalene could not be completely removed from the New Testament, because she seemed to play too important a role in Jesus' life. She is mentioned several times in the canonical gospels, and her prominence is indicated by the fact that her name almost always appears first in a list of women. Jesus' closeness to Mary Magdalene is further conveyed by the intensity of the scenes in which she appears. She is one of three women, including Jesus' mother, who stands by Jesus and watches as he is crucified. Later, these women courageously return to the tomb to anoint Jesus' body. And when they—or she—find the tomb empty, Mary Magdalene becomes the first person to confront the disappearance of Jesus' body and to express the resurrection of his soul—that is, to narrate the continuity of Being.

Given the centrality of this role, you would think that Mary Magdalene would be respected, even venerated, in the traditions. Just as Mary, Jesus' mother, gave birth to his body, Mary, Jesus' companion, must give birth to his story—the testament of energetic resurrection and eternal life. But the male disciples don't believe her; they have to see Jesus' spirit with their own eyes. Such disbelief is simply human; it is the institutionalization of what can and cannot be seen that is suspect.

As the early church elevated the Mother Mary to a being *above* other humans, so it damned Mary Magdalene to a being *beneath*. At the end of the sixth century, Pope Gregory the Great decreed that three New Testament Marys were the same woman—Mary Magdalene, Mary, the sister of Martha of Bethany, and the unnamed woman "who was a sinner" mentioned in Luke 7:37. He then combined these with a fourth woman, "the woman taken in adultery," to declare that the woman who anointed Jesus had "previously used the unguent to perfume her flesh in forbidden acts." Thus, Mary Magdalene became known as a prostitute rather than Jesus's wife, the partner and disciple clear-sighted and beloved enough to explain his understanding of the spirit. Rome repealed this characterization in 1969, admitting that it was scripturally inaccurate, but the damage was done. Mary Magdalene has lived on in consciousness as a fallen woman, her spiritual and psychic power misconstrued as promiscuity.

Mary Magdalene's marginalization in the Bible denied us a portrait of a strong, shamanic woman. It subjugated her to male dominance, and robbed us of an understanding of female spiritual power. It also eradicated a vision of sacred relationship between a divinely inspired male and female. In this way, it severely limited the ways the spirit could be seen and understood, while supporting the systematic subjugation of women in religion and society. But all this is changing. Again and again in the Gnostic texts, Jesus says, "those who have eyes, let them see, those who have ears, let them hear," reminding us that new tiers of consciousness are always available to those who seek openly.

Today, more and more of us are developing attentive relationships to intuition, to what the Gnostics called "knowledge of the heart." And this democratization of spirituality has released a massive longing for women's wisdom and historical examples of the sacred feminine. And because the physical and spiritual worlds are part of the same whole, we are also unearthing increasing physical evidence of Mary Magdalene's importance to Christianity, including a salvaged text of teachings that were inspired by her and recorded in the first centuries after Christ's death. The Gospel of Mary was discovered at an antiquities market in Cairo in 1896 and first translated into English almost 100 years later, reaching general English readers in the final years of the twentieth century. The Gospels of Thomas and Philip, both of which refer to Mary Magdalene as Jesus's beloved, were discovered in 1945, when farmers unearthed a clay jar filled with papyrus codices in the desert at Nag Hammadi, Egypt. Finally, in 2012, Harvard researcher Karen King decoded an ancient fragment of papyrus referring to "Jesus's wife."

The Gnostic Gospel of Mary is far different from the canonical gospels. It does not take place during Jesus' lifetime, but afterward, when he appears to Mary and speaks from the radiance and redemption of his death. In their channeled dialogue, we see Mary Magdalene as a trusting soul and complex thinker who understands the connotations of resurrection and the energetic realities of being. They discuss everyone's potential return to the whole, the sacred union and healing of duality that is made possible by listening inward, and by trusting that space where individual intuition dovetails with the spiritual intelligence that informs the universe. "Allow no one to mislead you, saying 'Here it is!' or 'There it is!'" the Gospel of Mary Magdalene says. "For it is within you that the Son of Man dwells."[1]

The voice of this book bubbled up urgently within me. I know it is just one spring in a vast interconnected net of water, filling wells, irrigating brittle metaphors and making lives fertile again with meaning. European legend has always held that Mary Magdalene escaped to France after Jesus' crucifixion along with Sarah, their

---

[1] For translations of the Gospel, see *The Gospel of Mary Magdalene* by Jean-Yves Leloup (Inner Traditions, 2002) with its especially luminous commentary, or *The Gospel of Mary of Magdala*, by Karen King (Polebridge Press, 2003).

daughter.2 If this was the case, then the offspring from their offspring would likely have multiplied, their bloodlines branching all over the land like rivers, links of their DNA quite possibly at work now in you, or in me. This is an interesting idea, but the mystery of Mary Magdalene, like the mystery of her beloved, is most powerful when it includes both history and metaphor, body and spirit. It is not a physical, literal story, but an energetic reality, a version of consciousness and love that is available to all who have ears to hear and eyes to see. Mary's story tells us as much about the present as it does about the past, because it is *all* her story—the bits we can infer about her life, the excavated fragments of her attributed teachings, her condemnation and execution by the Orthodox church and, perhaps most importantly, her current resurrection in collective consciousness. Mary Magdalene invites us to acknowledge our own wisdom and seek our own way. And she challenges us to think not about bloodlines but about the energies of spirit that move through the blood and beyond it. We may visualize this dynamic spirit as water, dispersing itself endlessly in rain, tears, sea and breath, constantly changing form, passing from visible bodies to invisible vapors as it cycles through all people, places and times. This endless connection and reconnection is our inheritance. It is an ever-renewing invitation to love, and by loving, to become whole.

Rachel Jamison Webster
Chicago, IL

---

2 "It is said that [Mary Magdalene] lived in the caves that extend through Southern France and developed a kind of clairvoyance— 'clear seeing' — that permitted her to become intimate with the caverns and passageways without the use of torches. These caves, carved of water from the region's limestone, extend for hundreds of miles and make up the most subterranean system in the world. . .Mary is said to have lived the last thirty years of her life in intimate connection with this hidden part of the earth," write David Tresemer and Laura Lea-Cannon, in the Preface to *The Gospel of Mary Magdalene,* translated by Jean-Yves LeLoup, Inner Traditions, 2002.

About the Author

Rachel Jamison Webster is author of the full-length collection of poetry, *September* (TriQuarterly, 2013) and the cross-genre book, *The Endless Unbegun* (Twelve Winters, 2015). Her essays and poems appear in many journals and anthologies, including *Tin House, Poetry, The Southern Review, The Paris Review* and *Narrative*. She lives with her daughter Adèle in Evanston, IL, where she teaches poetry and directs the Creative Writing Program at Northwestern University. You can read more about Rachel at www.racheljamisonwebster.com.

CPSIA information can be obtained
at www.ICGtesting.com
Printed in the USA
LVHW080200200219
608132LV00006B/144/P